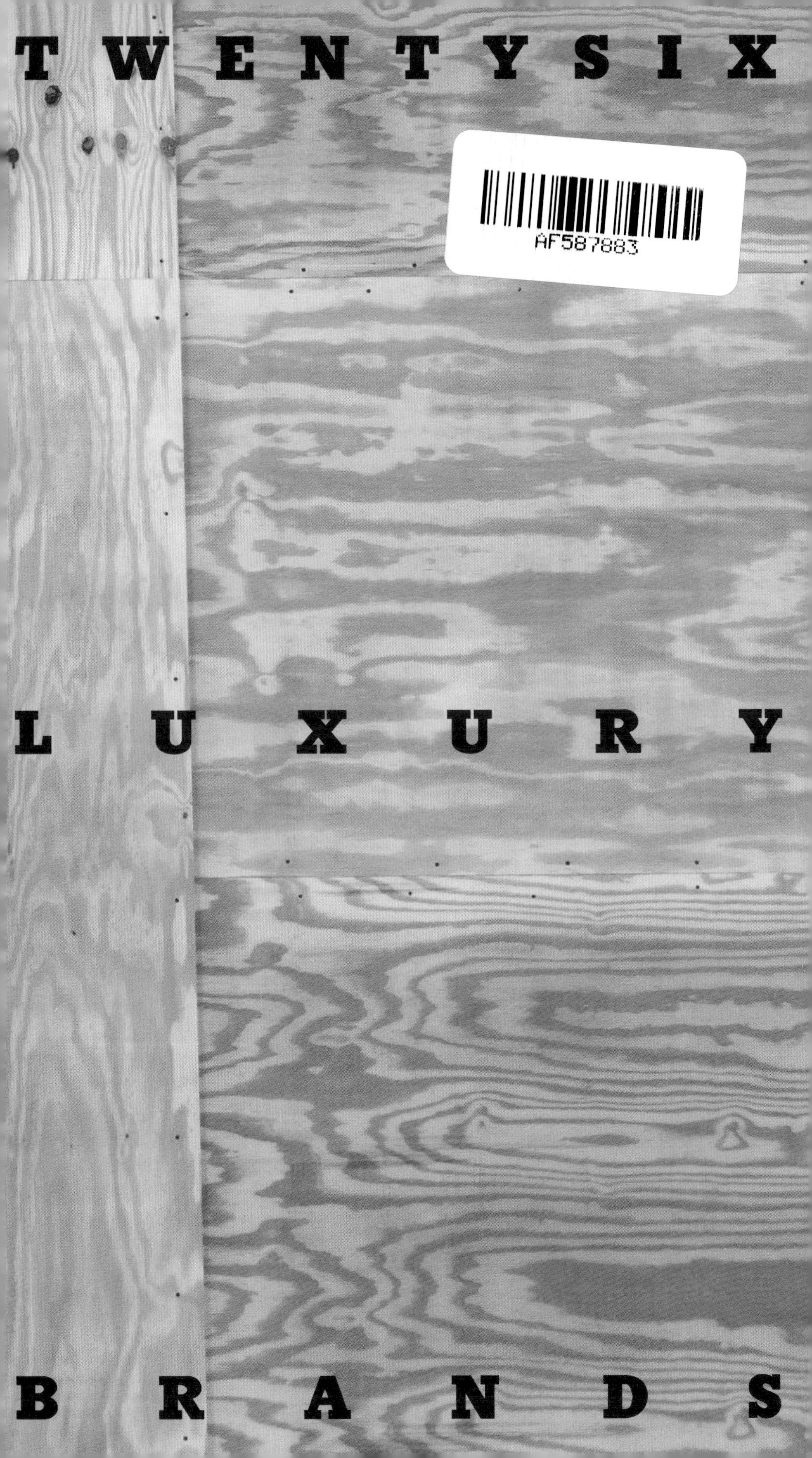
TWENTYSIX
LUXURY
BRANDS

TWENTYSIX LUXURY BRANDS

*

ELECTION WEEK

NOV 2020

NEW YORK CITY

*

MARIEVIC

Clothes cannot be closed. Not entirely. This is perhaps a stupid point, but like all stupid points, may be profitably pointed out. There are closures for clothes, zippers and buttons, straps and such, but still, they must be necessarily open, allowing room for the appropriate appendage, or in the case of full bondage gear, breath. Yet what we want most from clothes is closure, physical and psychoanalytical. Cuddly comfort or strict uniform, it's all the same, the desire to be well-suited, set out and set apart, fit for purpose and occasion. I am I because my little togs know me. But again, the failure of my stupid face sticking out, ripe for slapping, the problem of my hands, solved by pocketing. We wear our fragility on the outside. Like cops with a big gun on a breakable hip, or a thick diamond choker, which states the obvious, our porousness is betrayed by our props. And this too may be the point, the flesh wanting its betrayal, asking to be saved.

Vanessa Place

November 6, 2020 1:44 PM
620 Madison Ave, New York New York, 10022

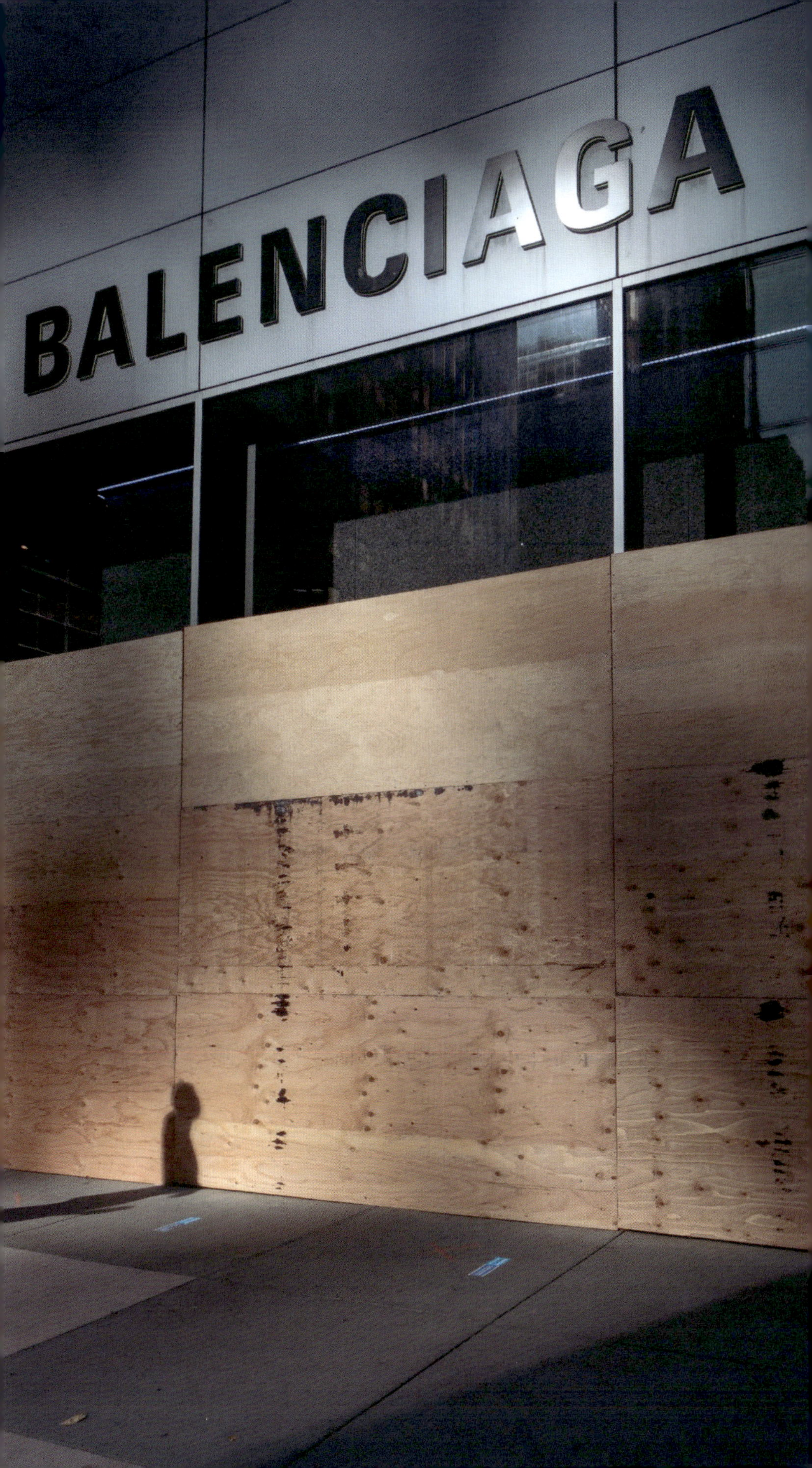
BALENCIAGA

November 5, 2020 1:11 PM
99 Prince Street, New York New York, 10012

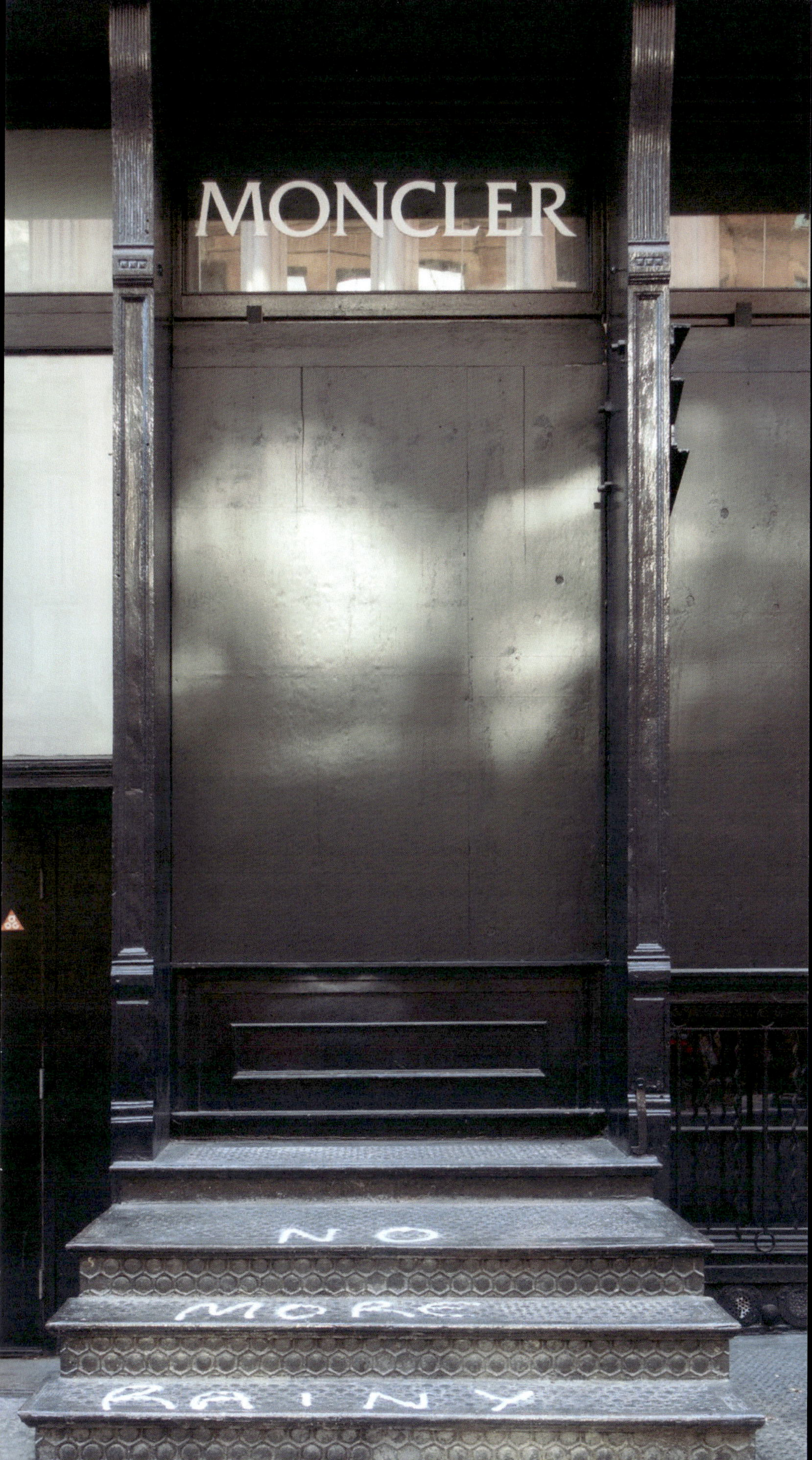
MONCLER
NO
MORE
RAINY

November 6, 2020 1:51 PM
650 Madison Ave, New York New York, 10022

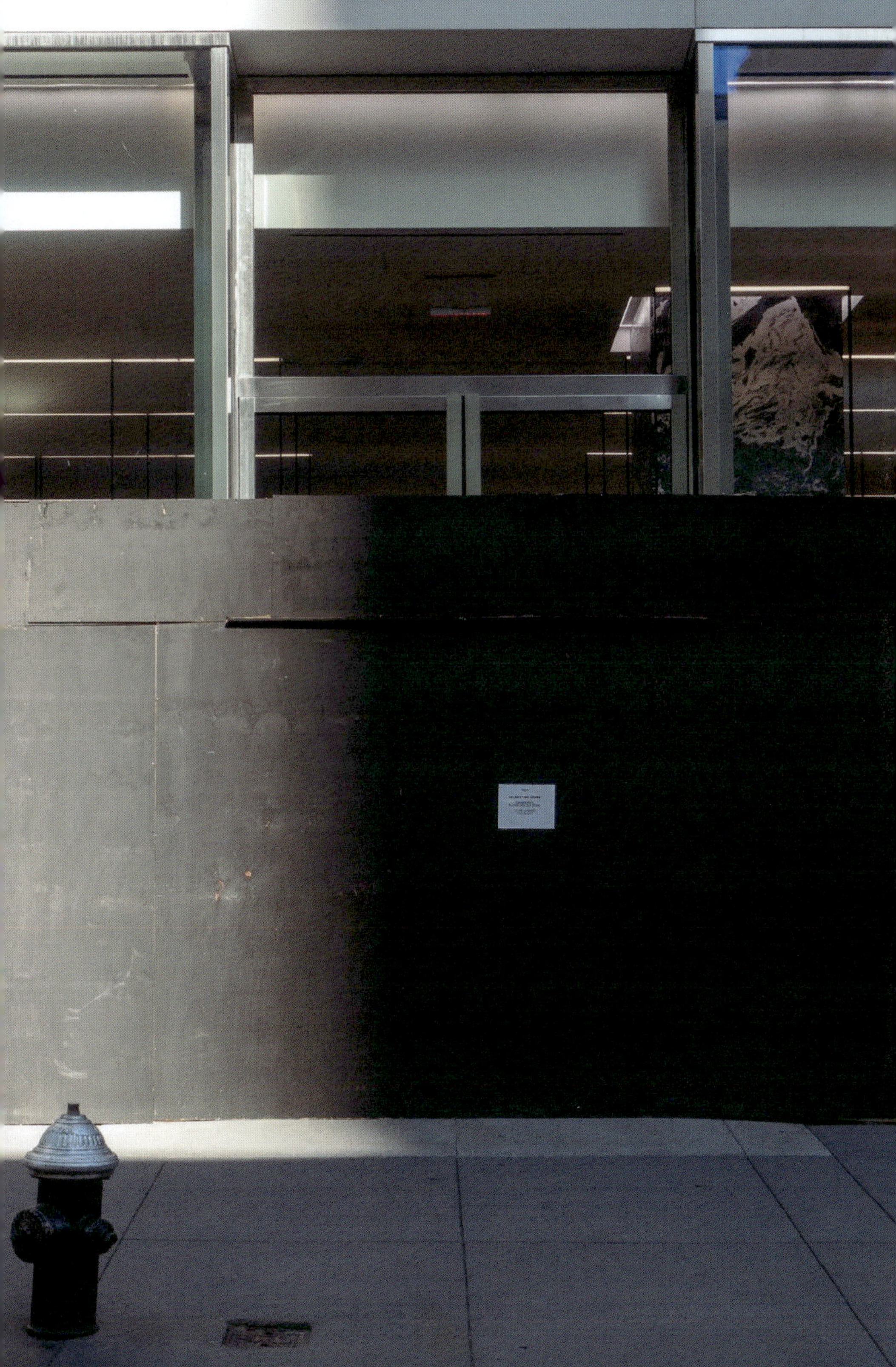
CELINE
PARIS

November 3, 2020 11:22 AM
611 Fifth Ave, New York New York, 10022

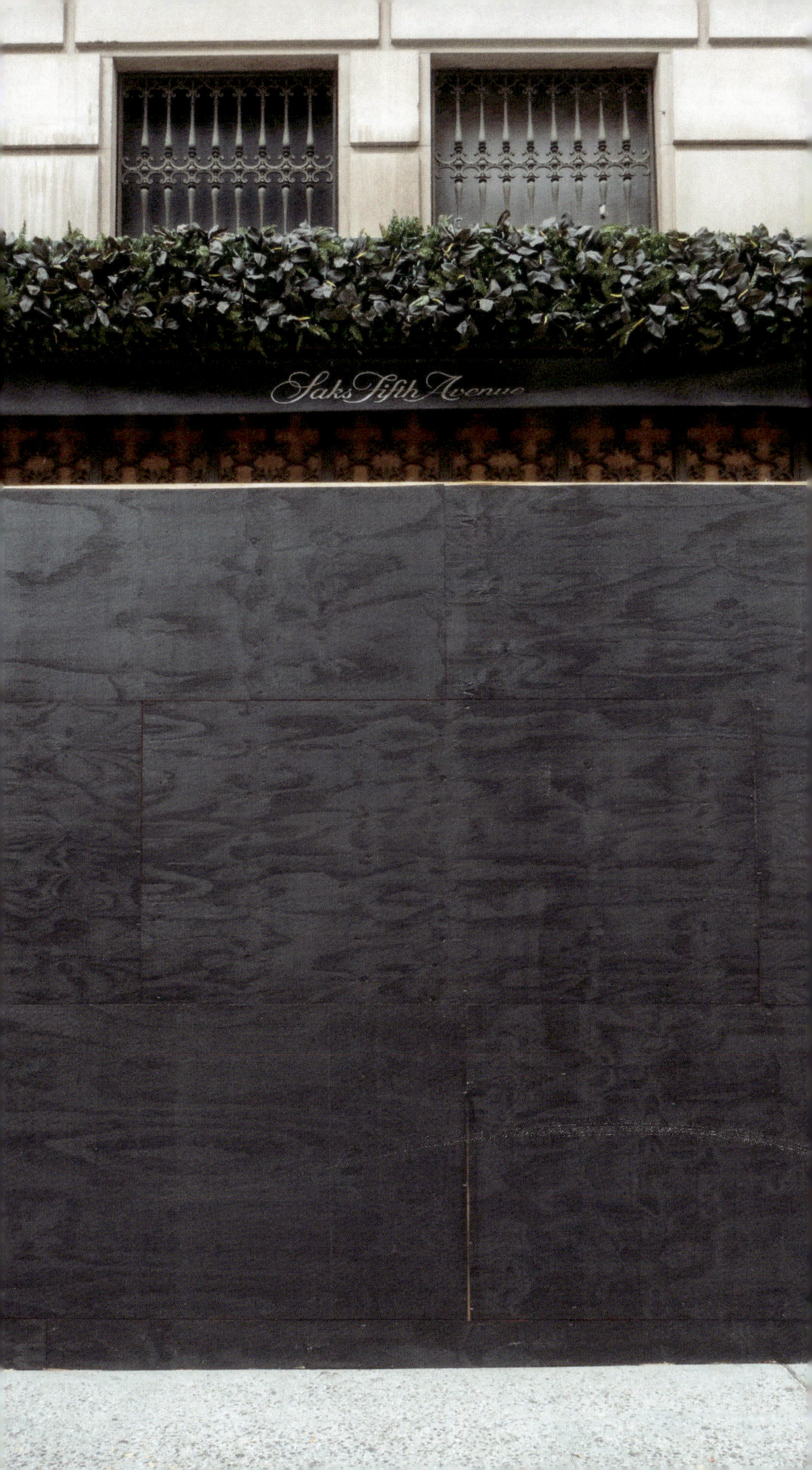
Saks Fifth Avenue

November 3, 2020 11:27 AM
510 Madison Ave, New York New York, 10022

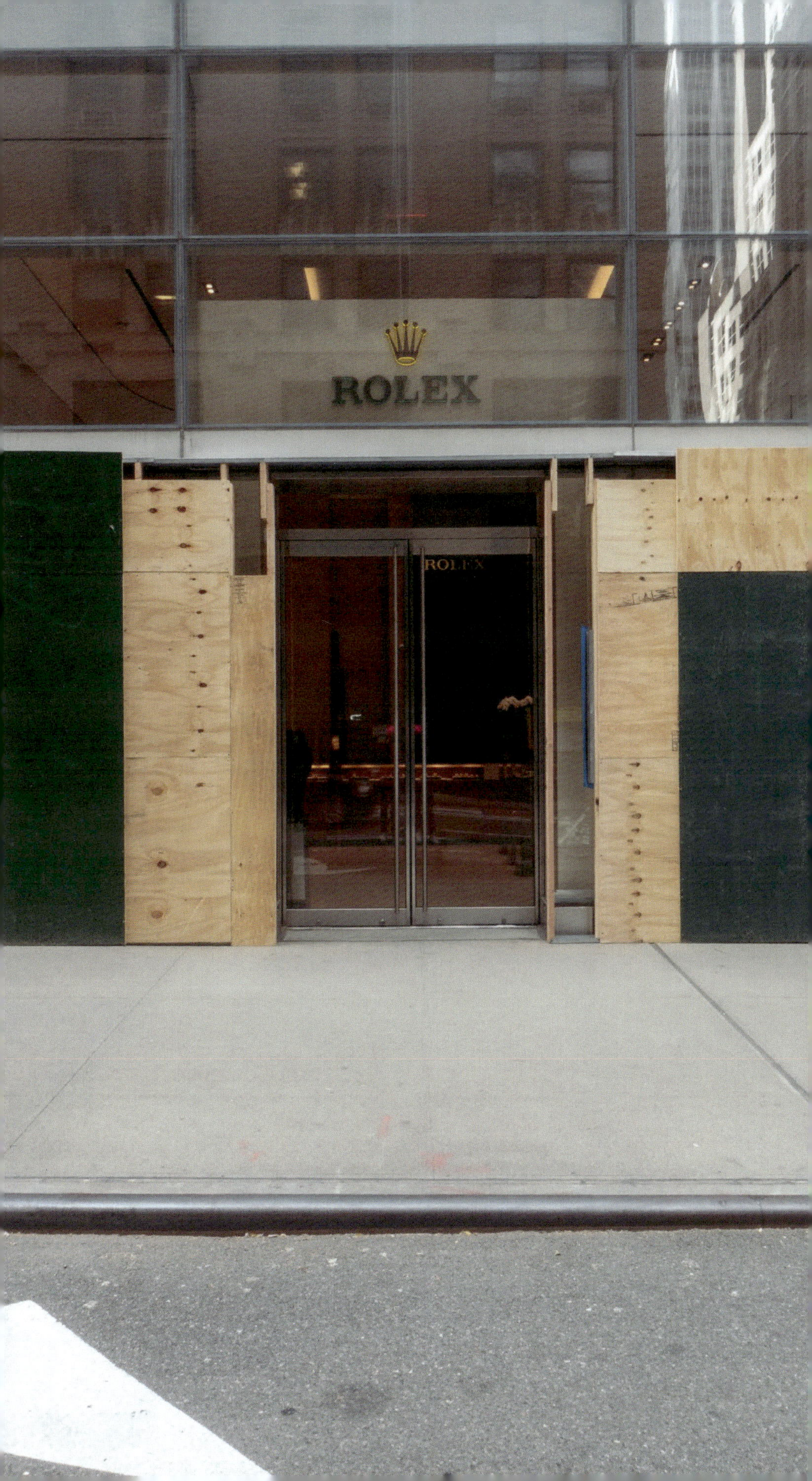
ROLEX
ROLEX

November 3, 2020 11:37 AM
827 Madison Ave, New York New York, 10022

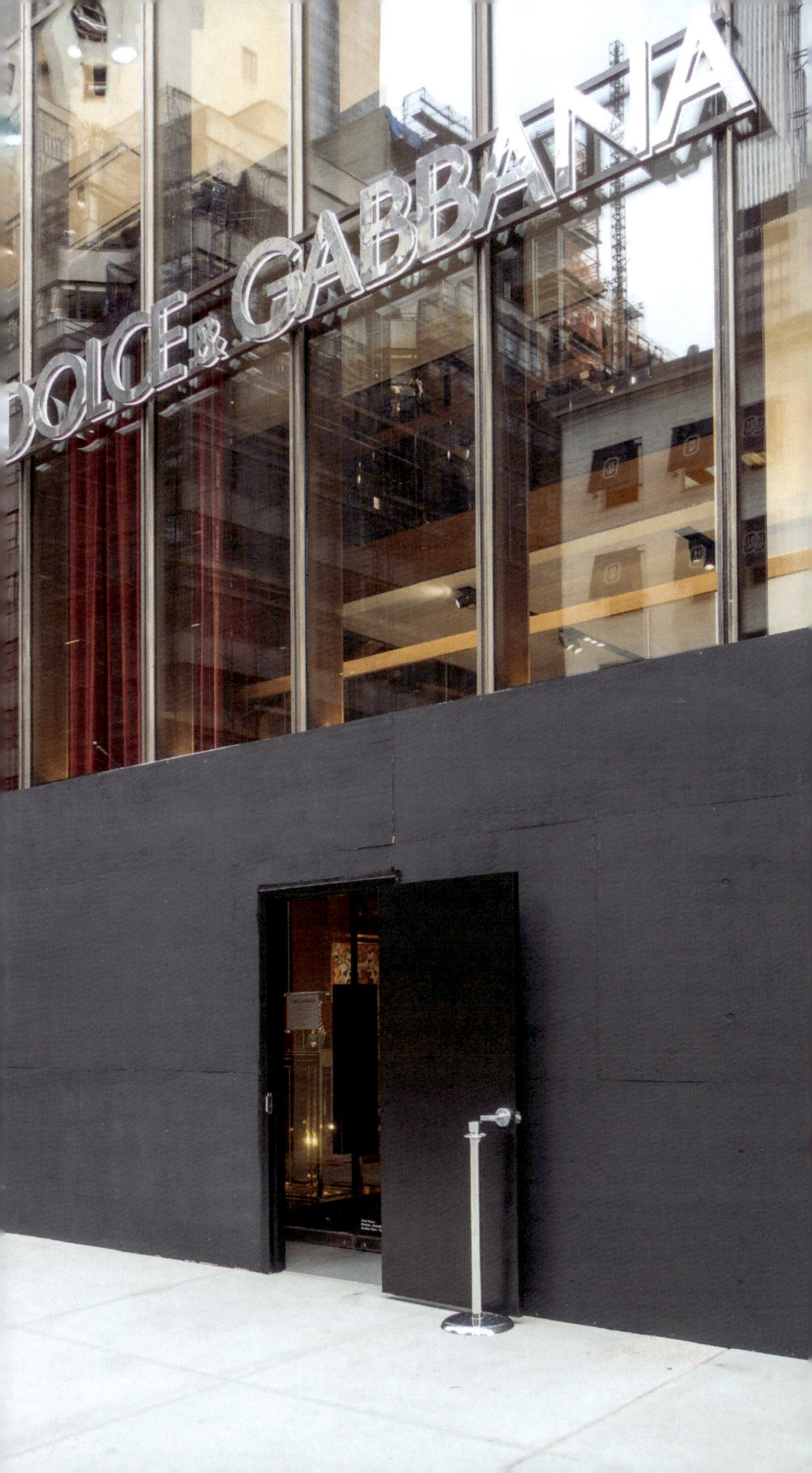
DOLCE & GABBANA

November 4, 2020 1:44 PM
3 E. 57th Street, New York New York, 10022

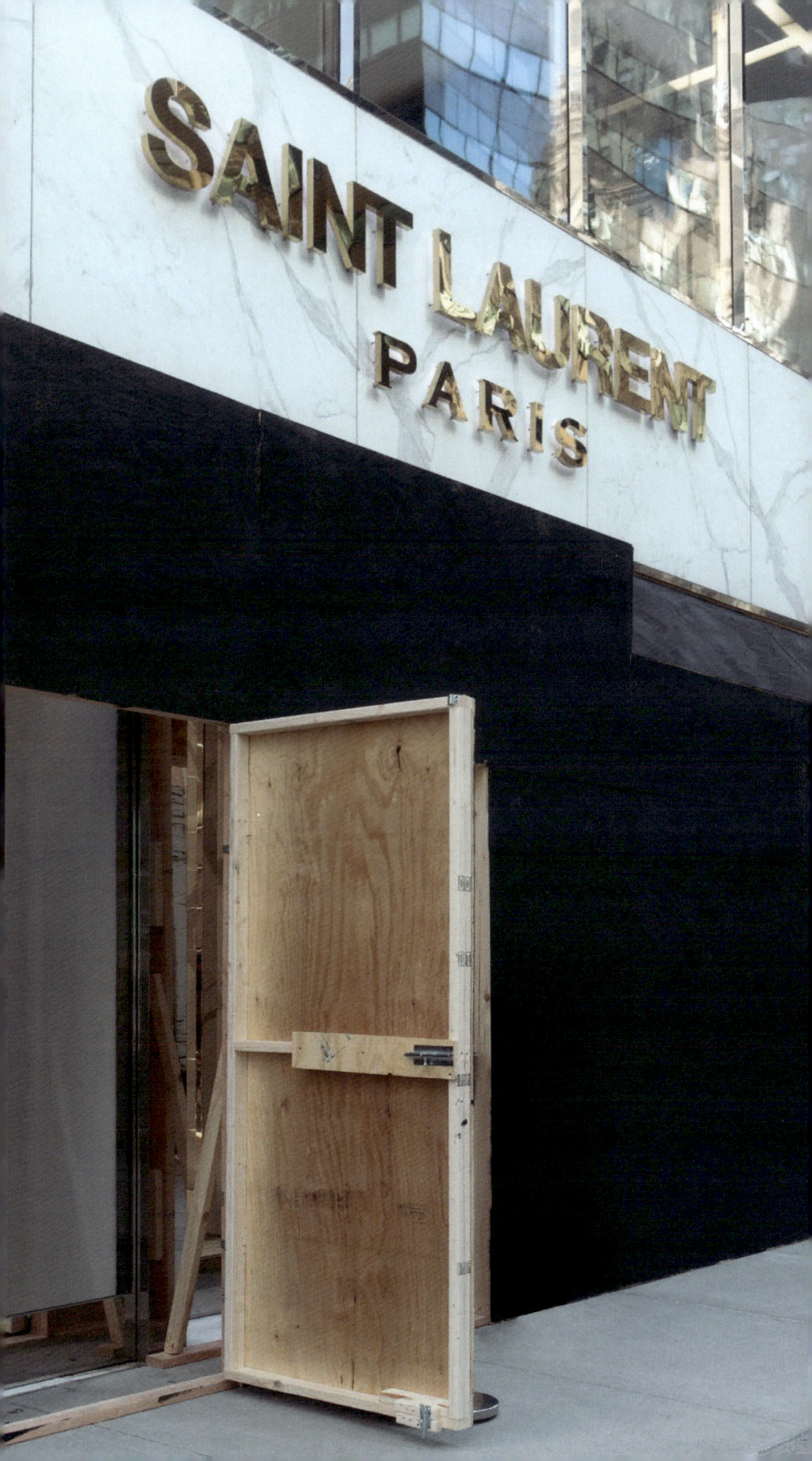
SAINT LAURENT
PARIS

November 3, 2020 1:55 PM
754 Fifth Ave, New York New York, 10019

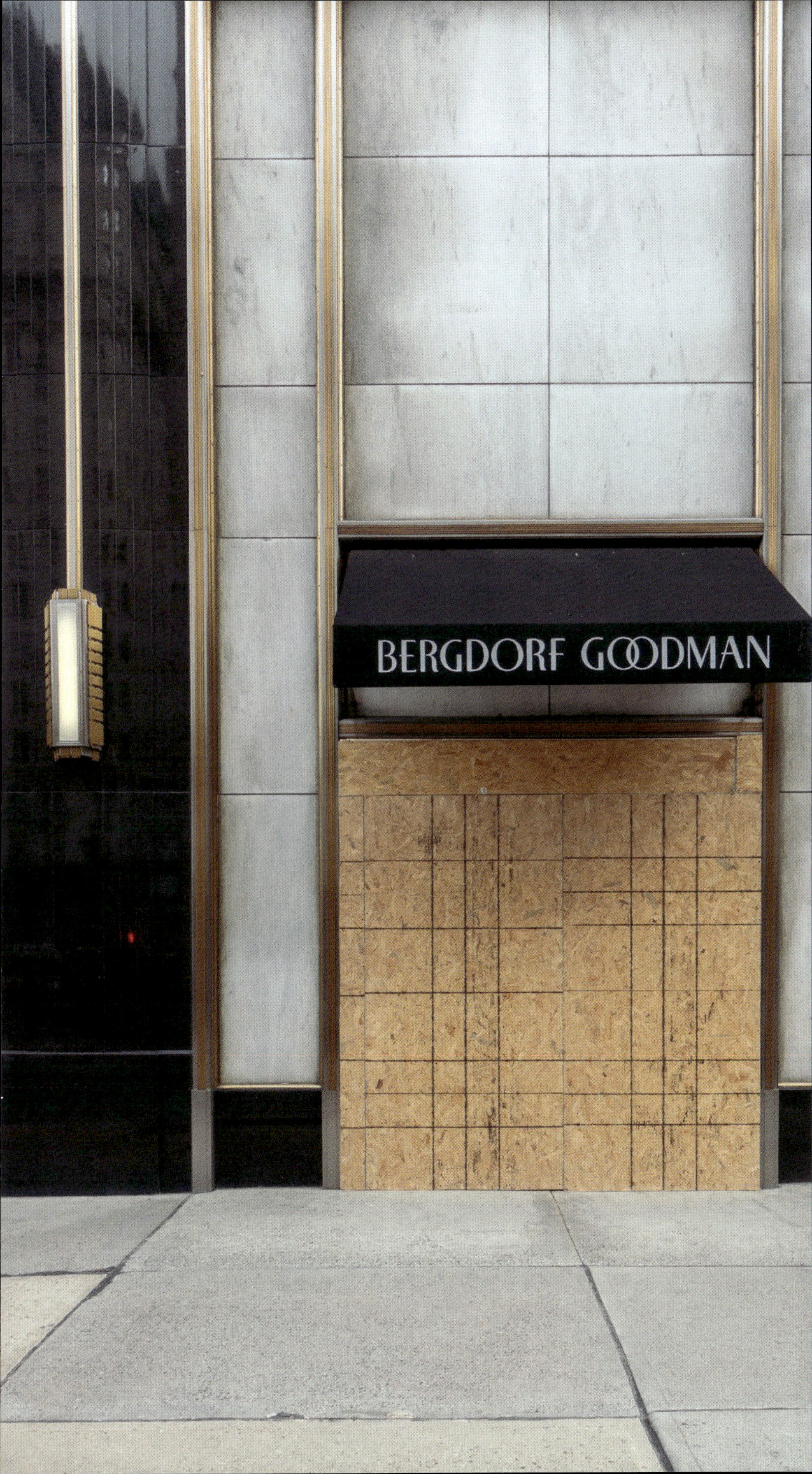
BERGDORF GOODMAN

November 3, 2020 1:58 PM
743 Fifth Ave, New York New York, 10022

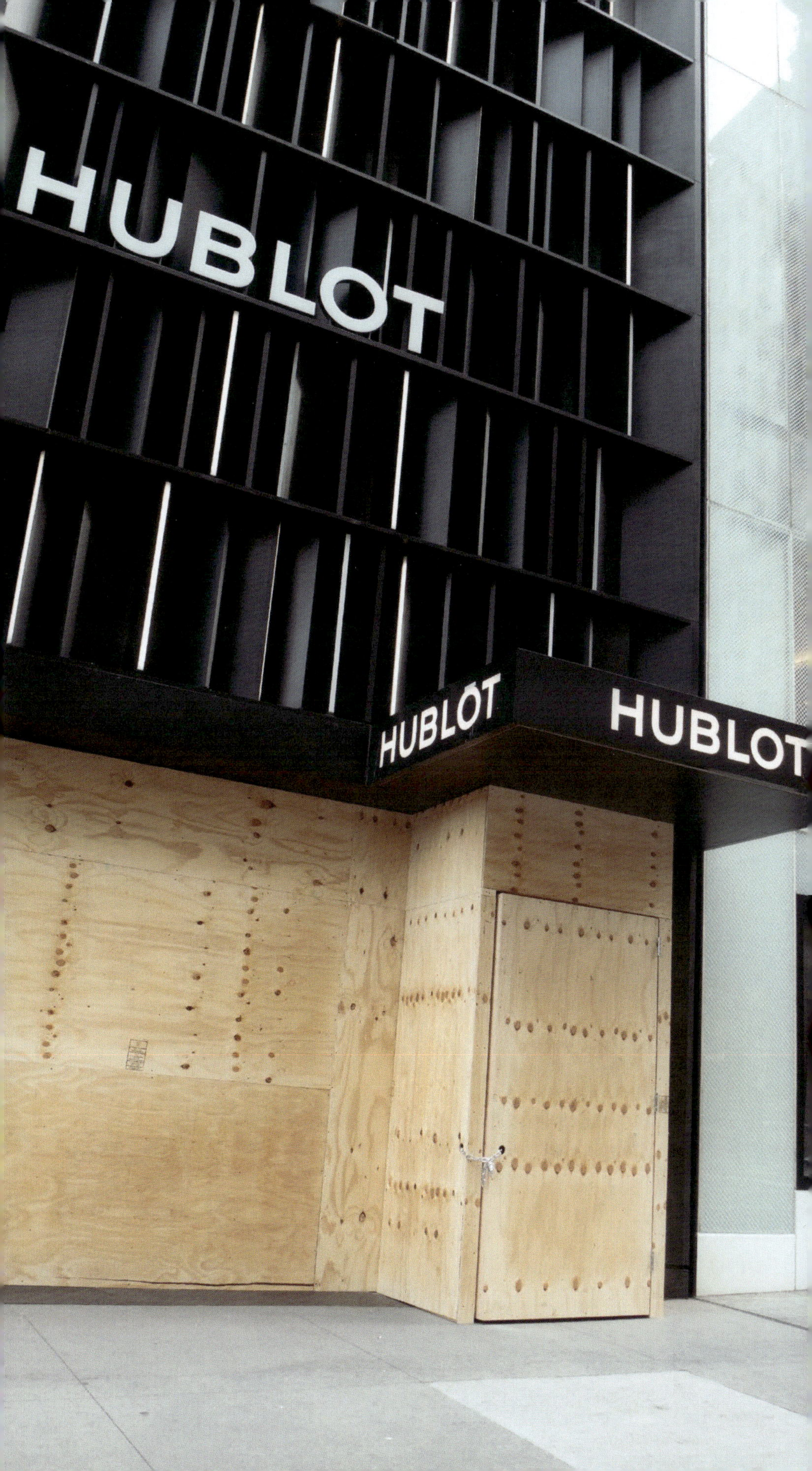
HUBLOT
HUBLOT
HUBLOT

November 3, 2020 1:31 PM
15 E 57th Street, New York New York, 10022

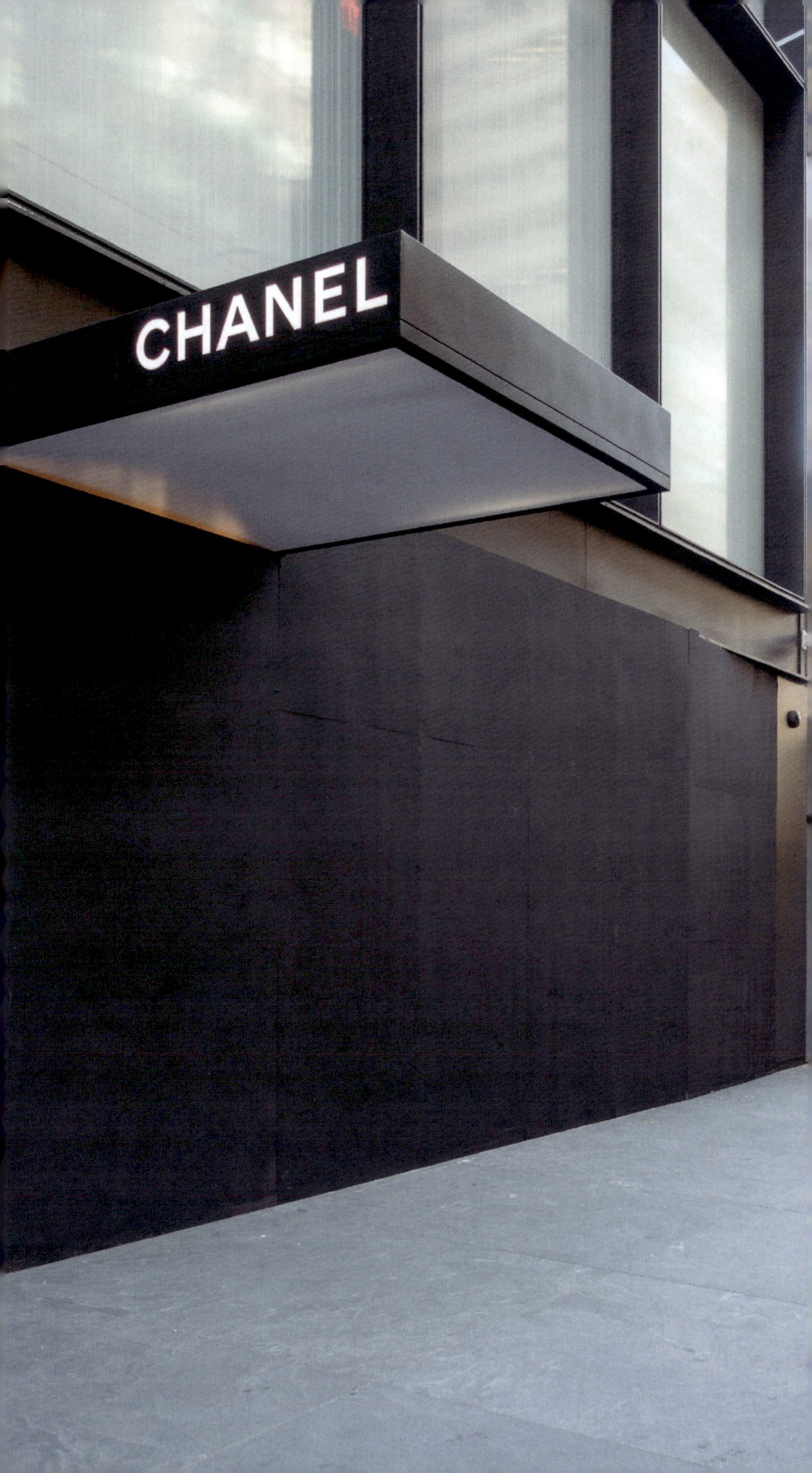
CHANEL

November 4, 2020 2:12 PM
21 E 57th Street, New York New York, 10022

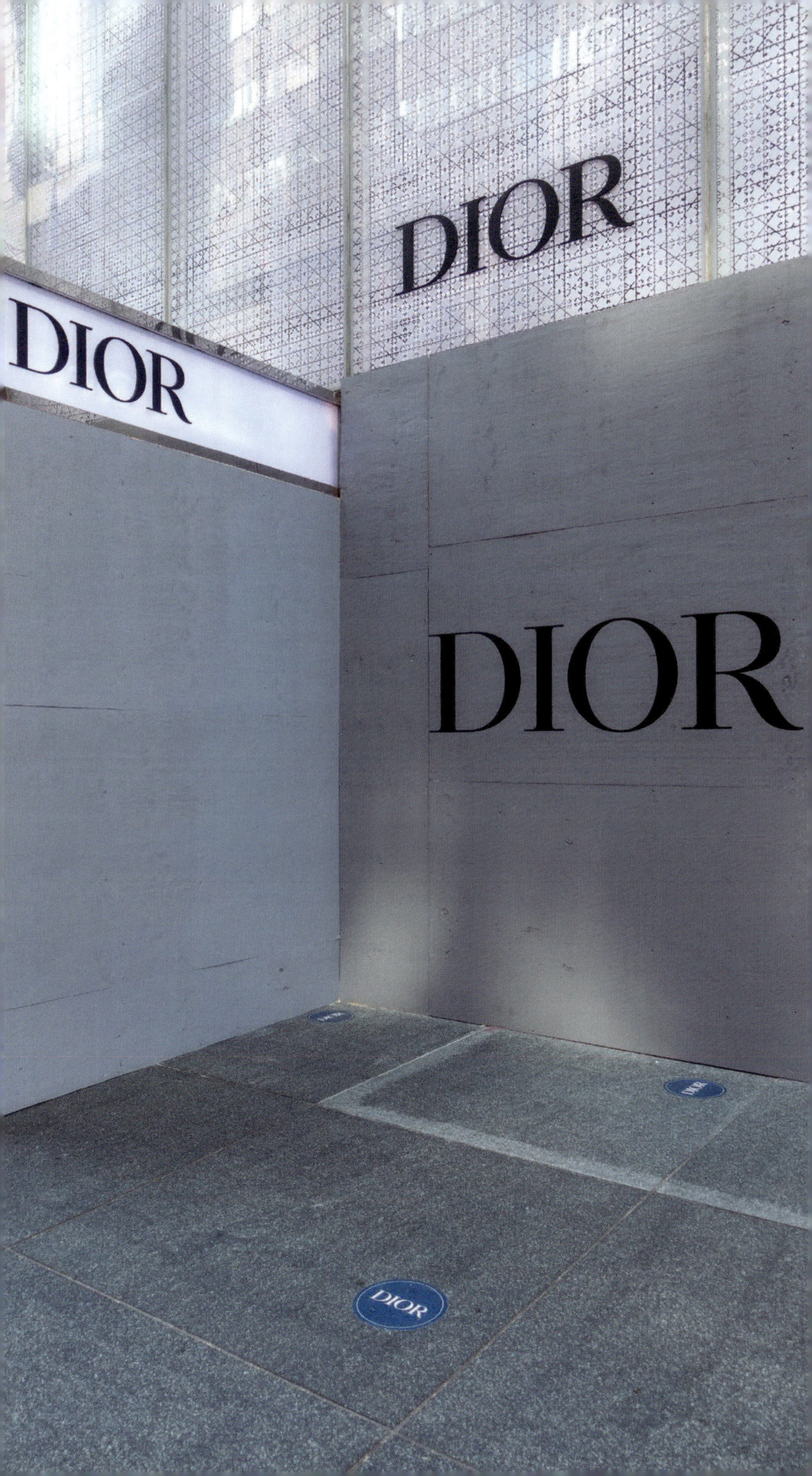

DIOR

DIOR

DIOR

November 3, 2020 12:01 PM
9 E 57th Street, New York New York, 10022

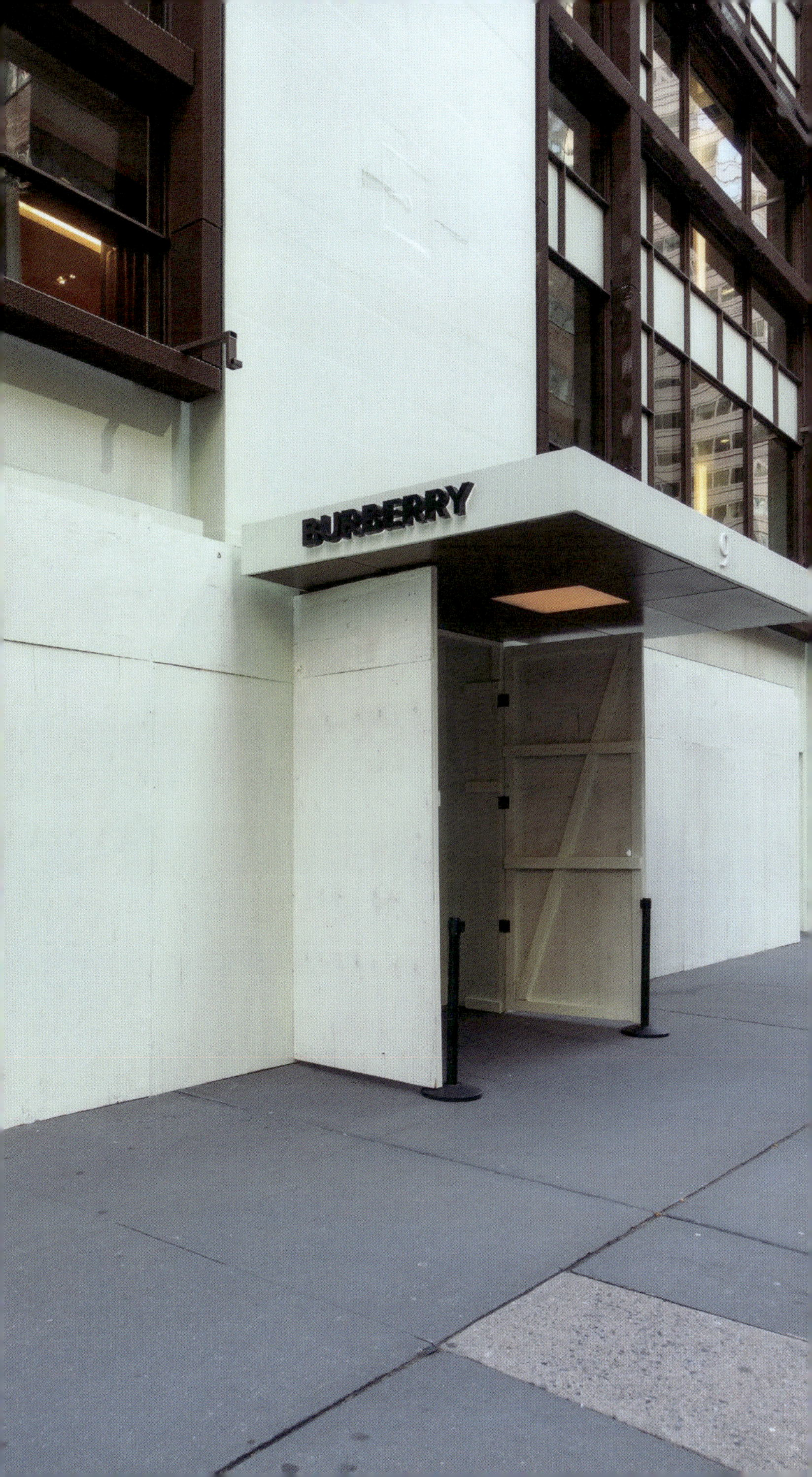
BURBERRY

November 5, 2020 2:12 PM
79 Greene Street, New York New York, 10012

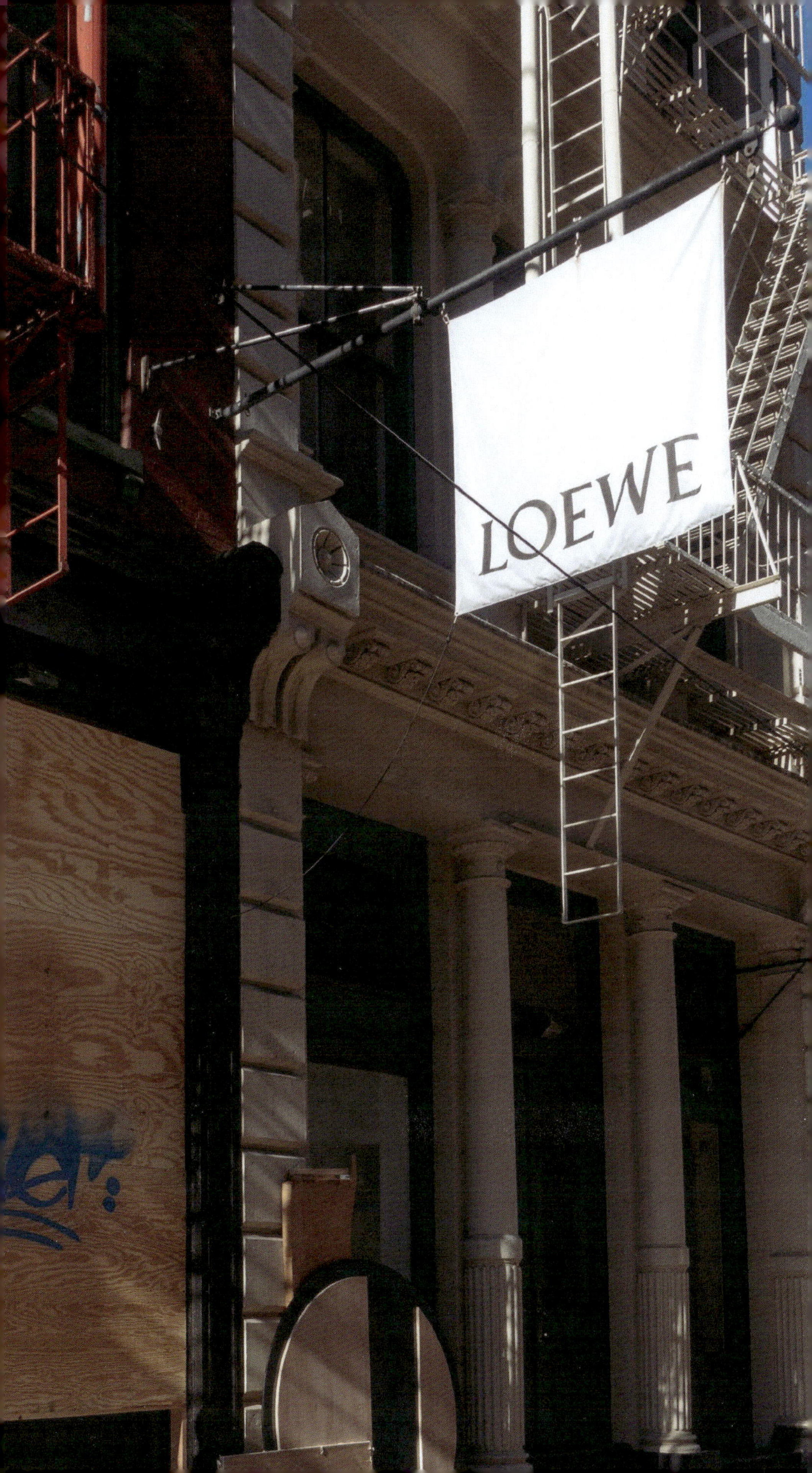
LOEWE

November 5, 2020 1:13 PM
111 Greene Street, New York New York, 10012

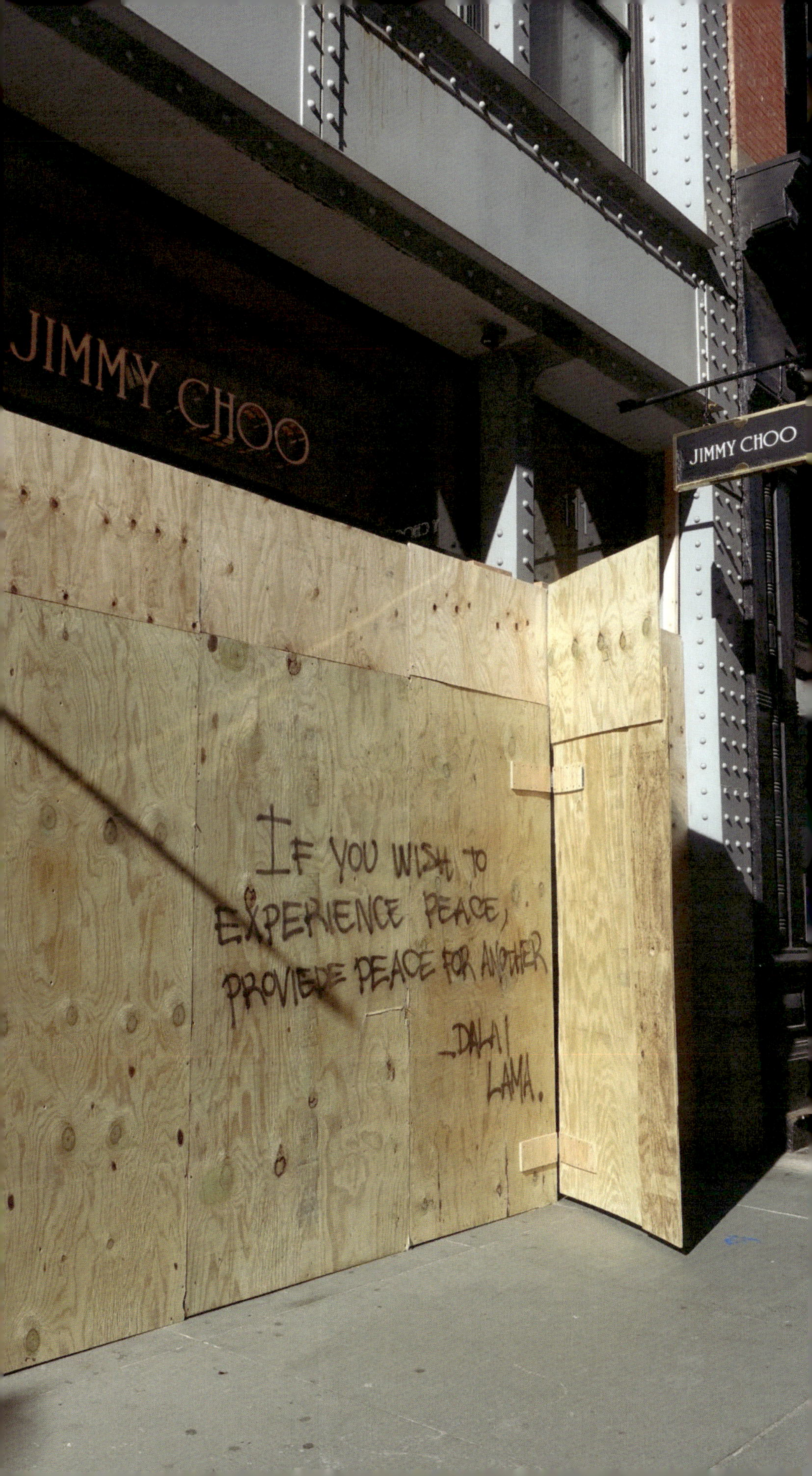
JIMMY CHOO
JIMMY CHOO
IF YOU WISH TO
EXPERIENCE PEACE,
PROVIDE PEACE FOR ANOTHER
-DALAI
LAMA.

November 5, 2020 1:23 PM
99 Prince Street, New York New York, 10012

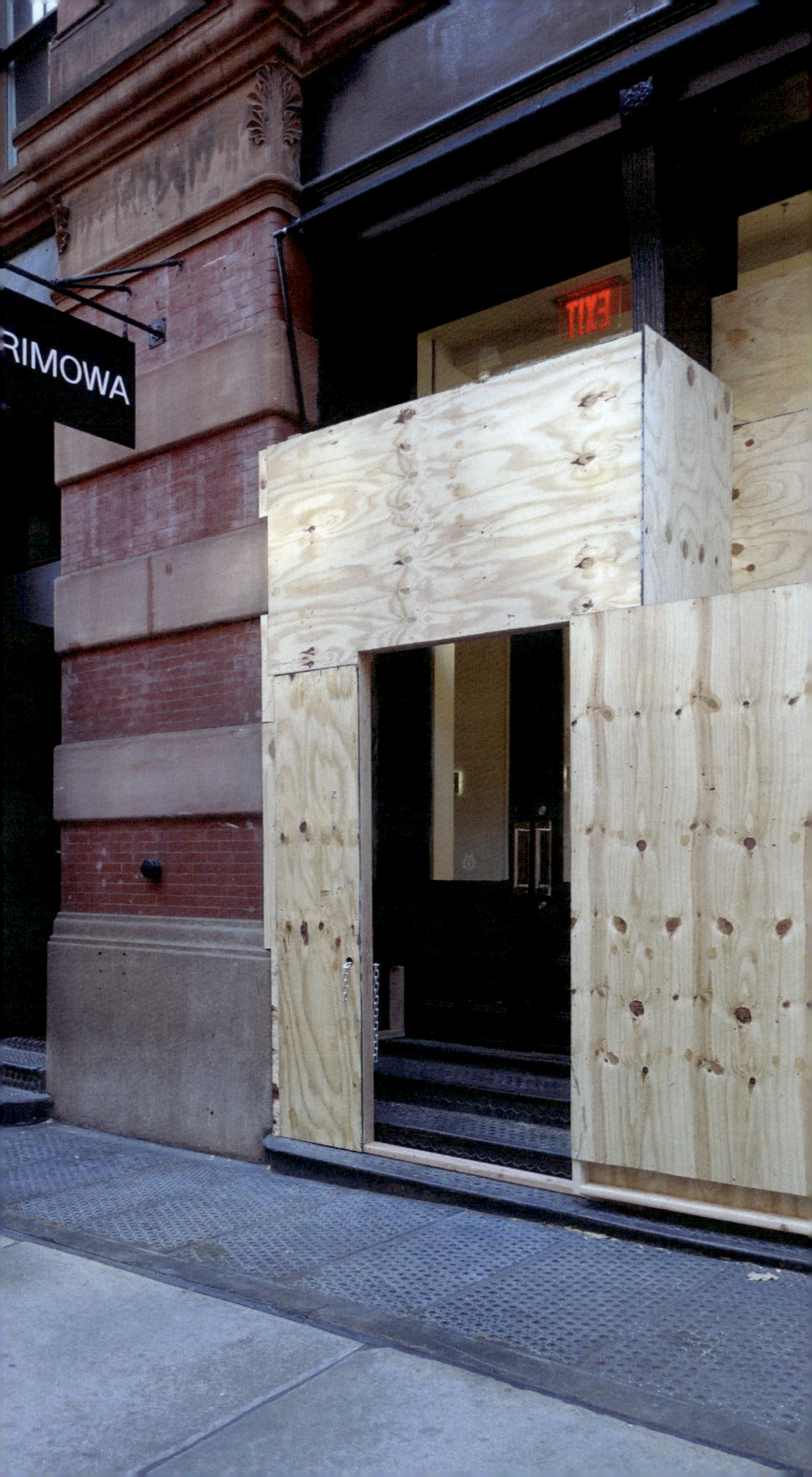
RIMOWA

November 5, 2020 12:23 PM
99 Greene Street, New York New York, 10012

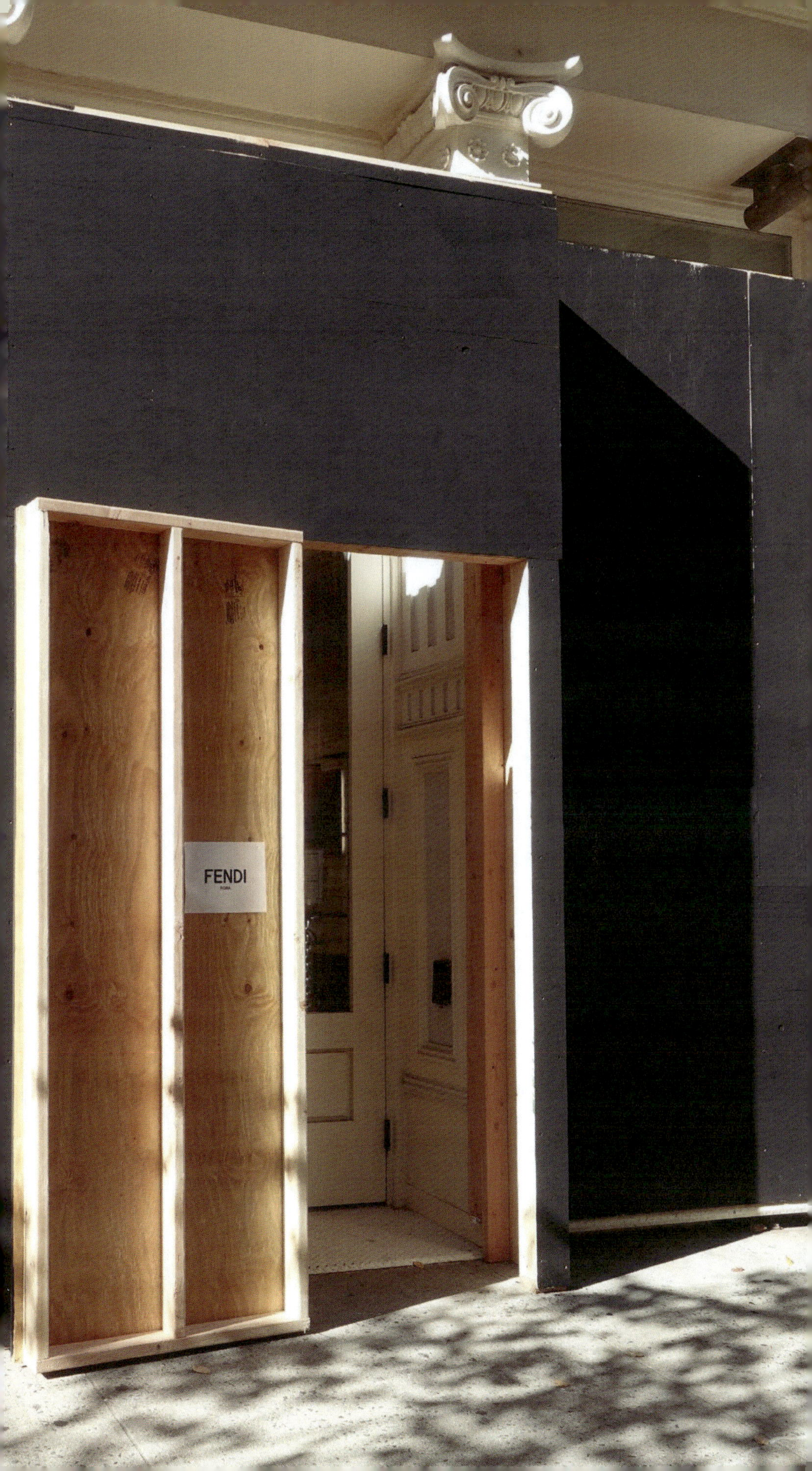
FENDI

November 5, 2020 1:27 PM
124 Prince Street, New York New York, 10012

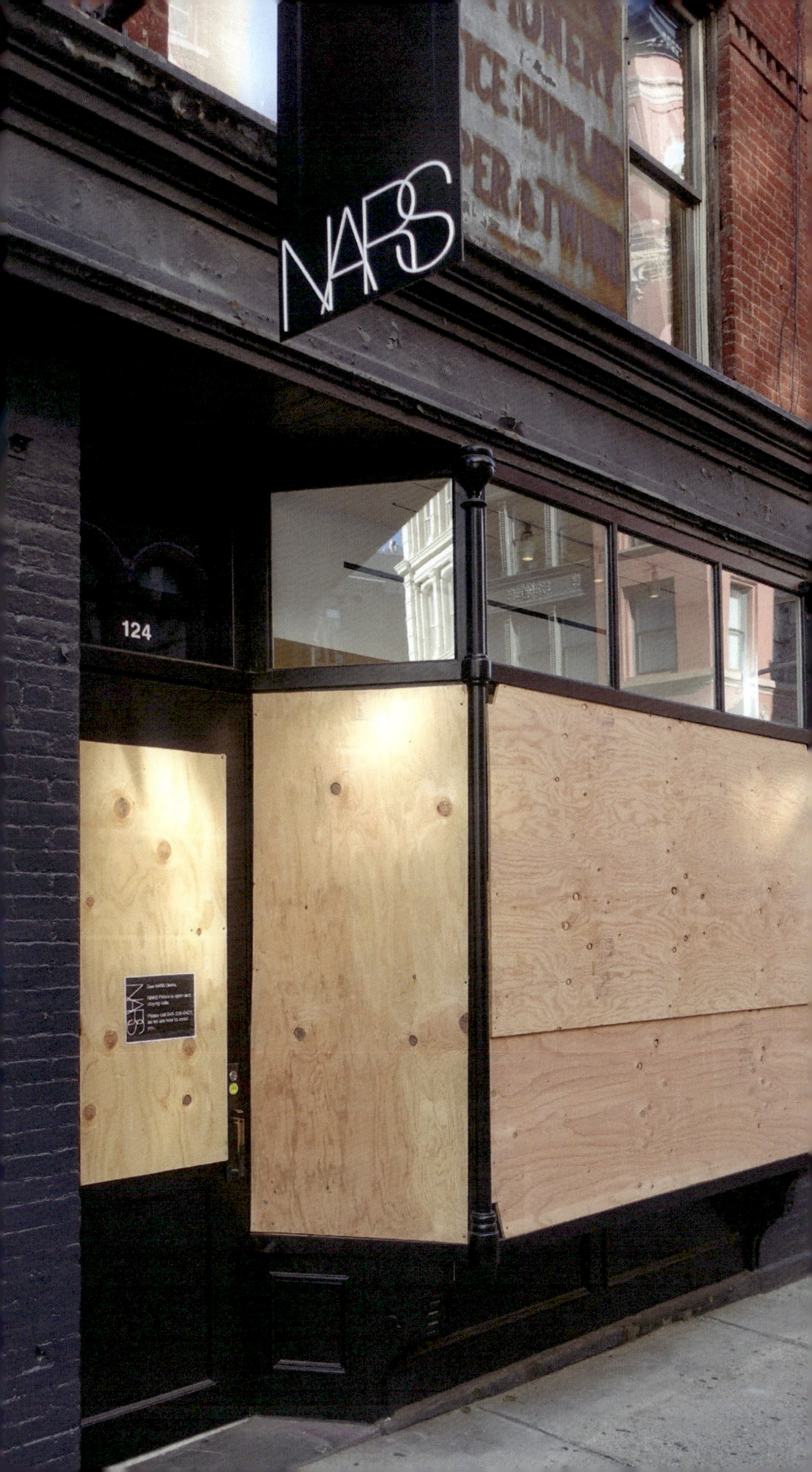
NARS
124
NARS

November 5, 2020 1:42 PM
71 Mercer Street, New York New York, 10012

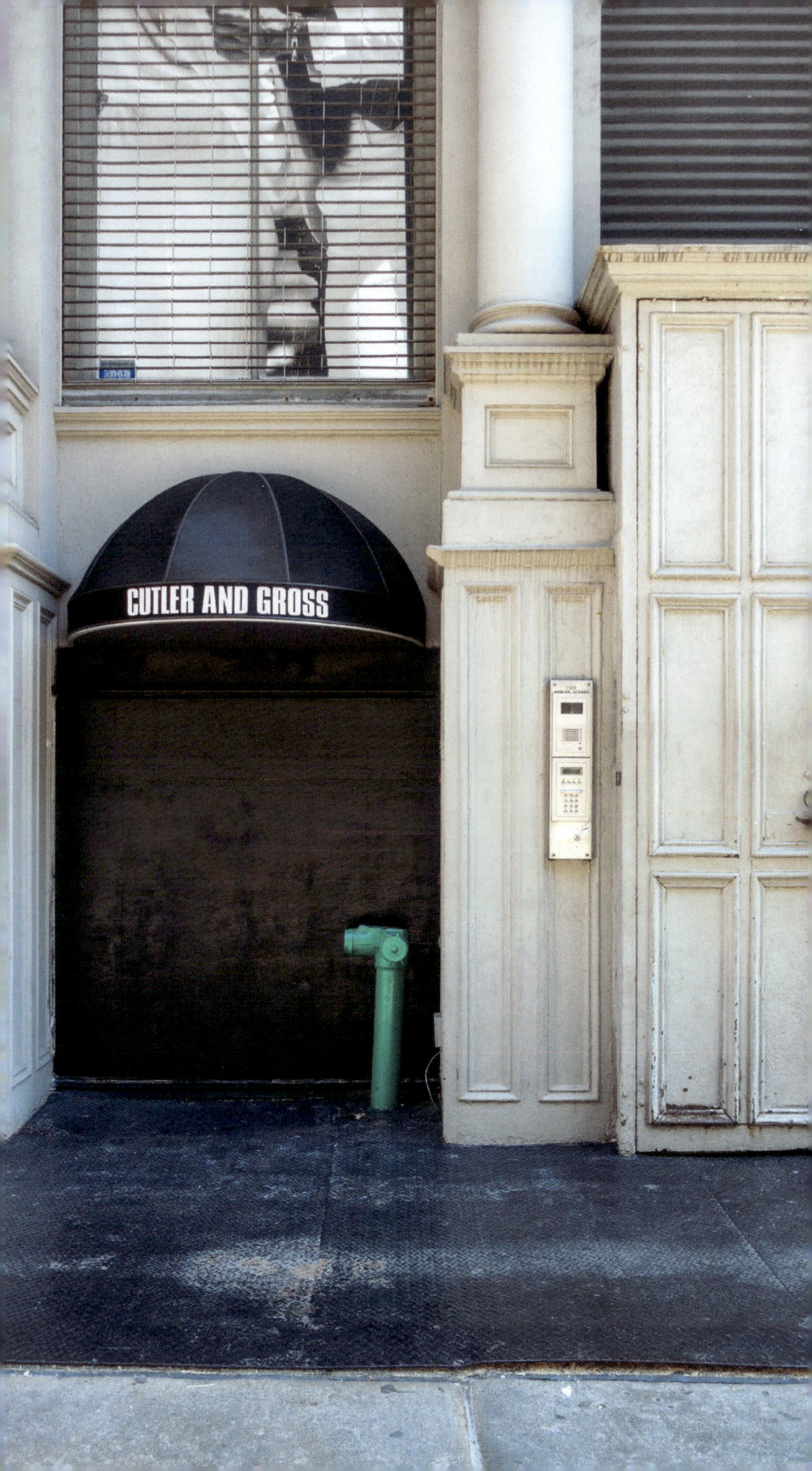
CUTLER AND GROSS

November 4, 2020 1:51 PM
744 Fifth Avenue, New York New York, 10019

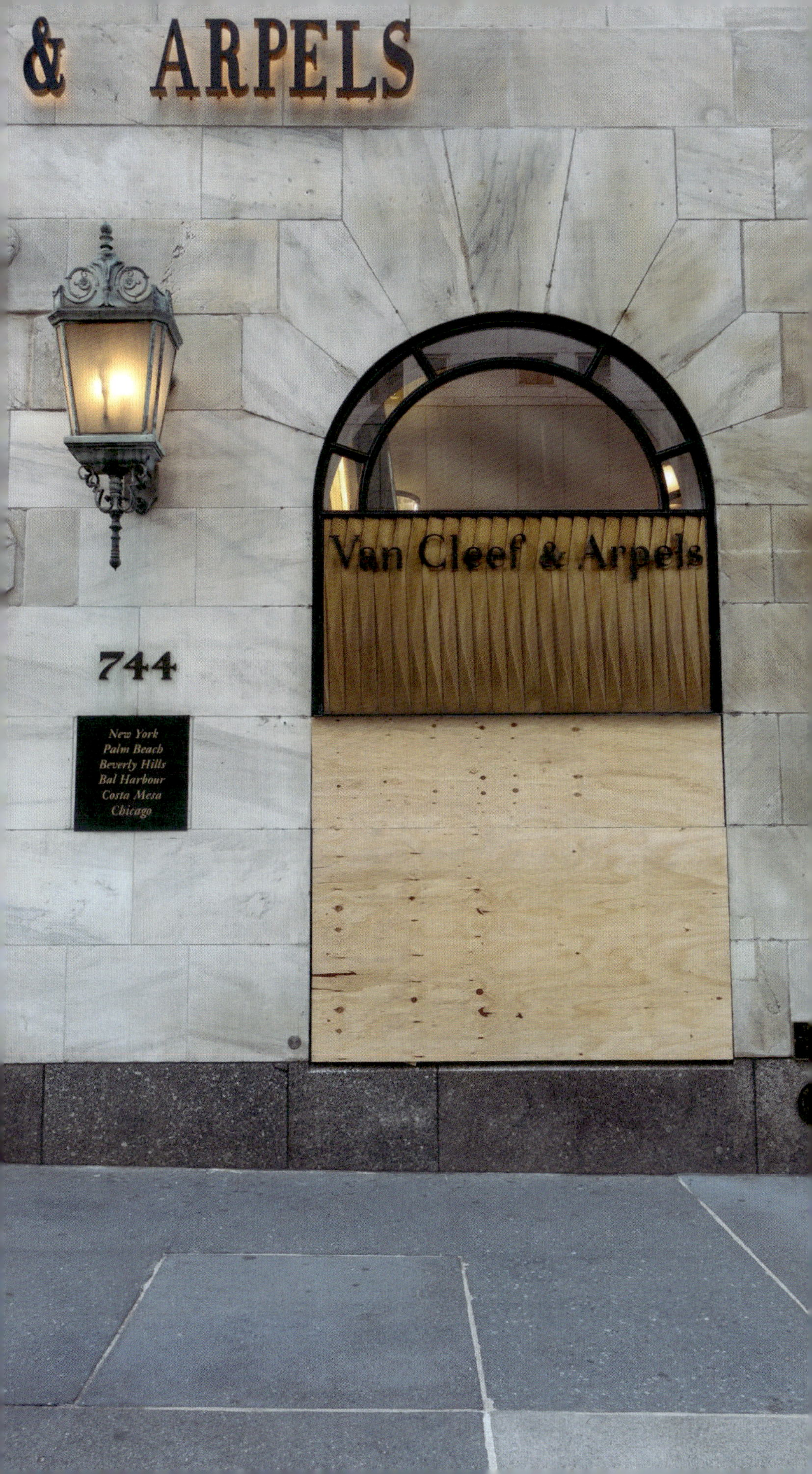

& ARPELS
Van Cleef & Arpels
744
New York
Palm Beach
Beverly Hills
Bal Harbour
Costa Mesa
Chicago

November 3, 2020 12:41 PM
655 Fifth Avenue, New York New York, 10022

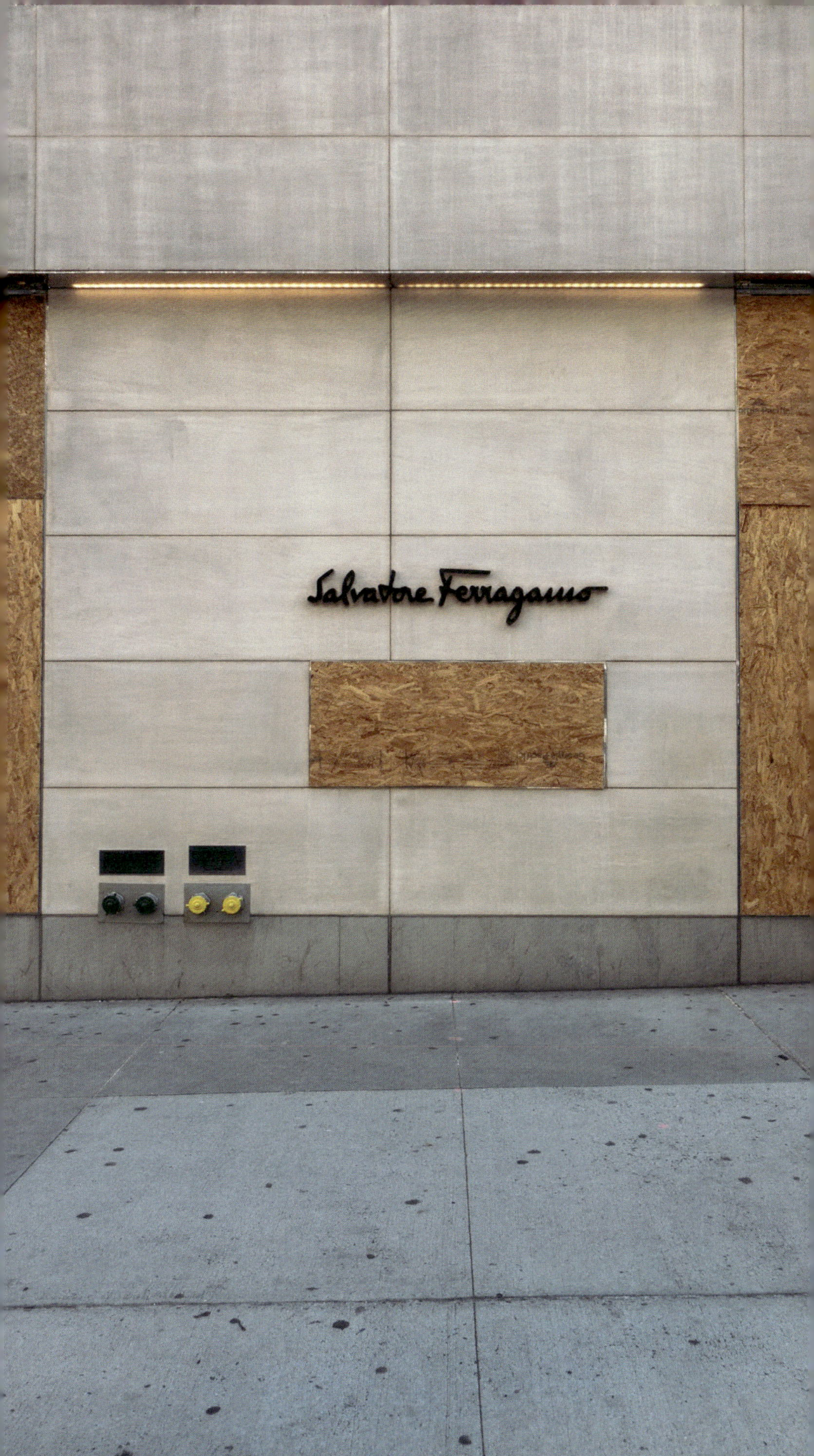
Salvatore Ferragamo

November 3, 2020 12:47 PM
653 Fifth Avenue, New York New York, 10022

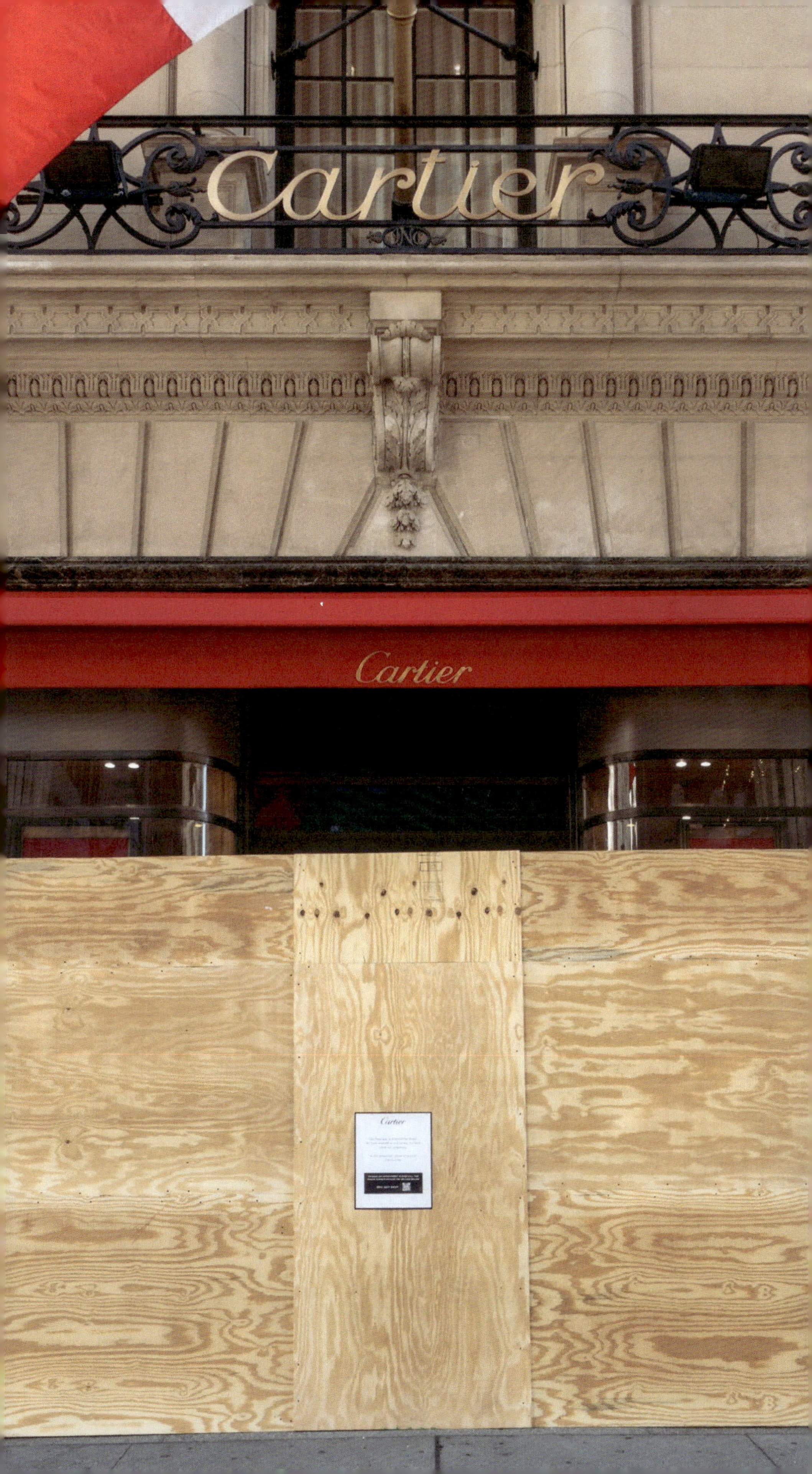
Cartier
Cartier
Cartier

November 3, 2020 12:32 PM
647 Fifth Avenue, New York New York, 10022

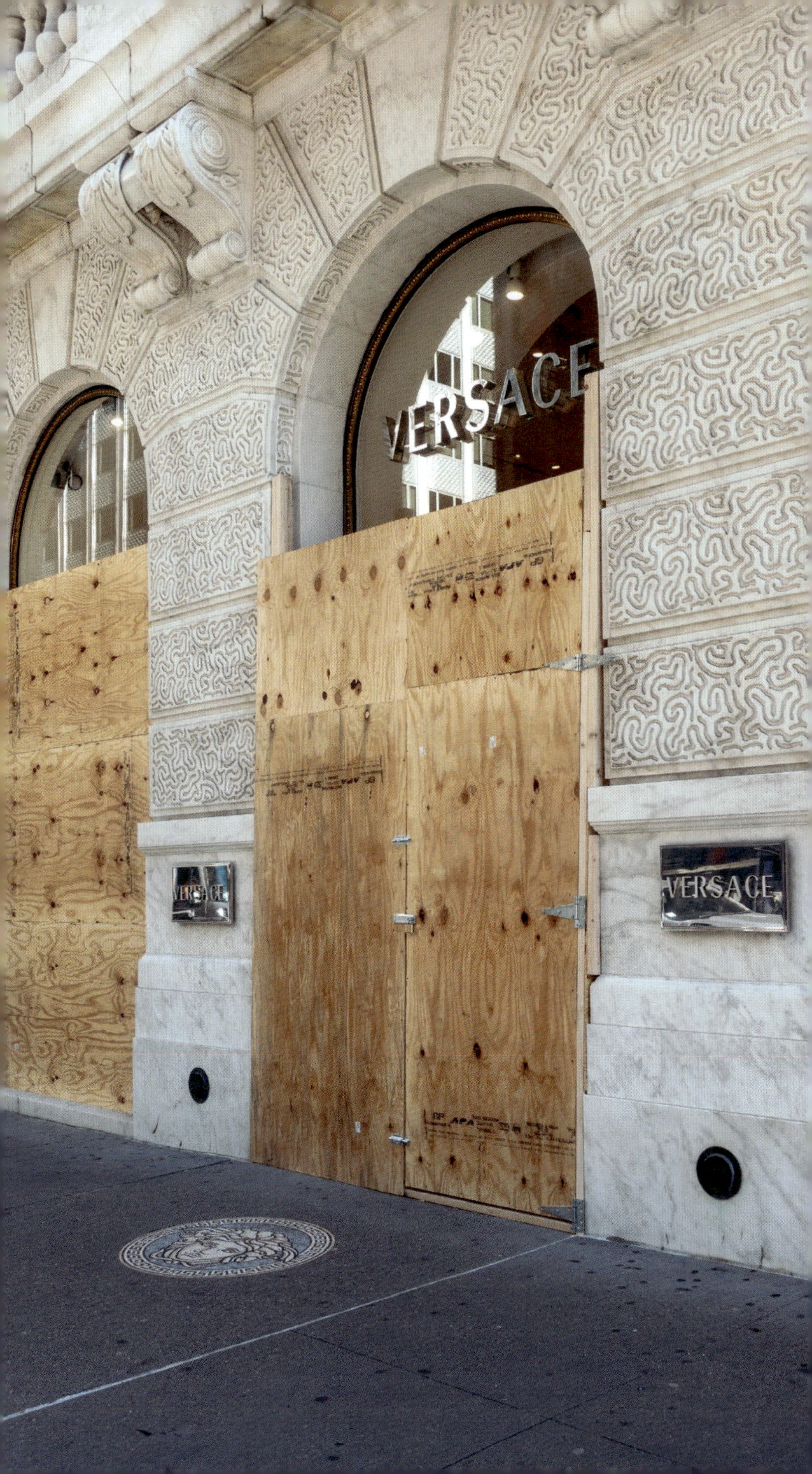
VERSACE
VERSACE
VERSACE

November 3, 2020 12:28 PM
645 Fifth Avenue, New York New York, 10022

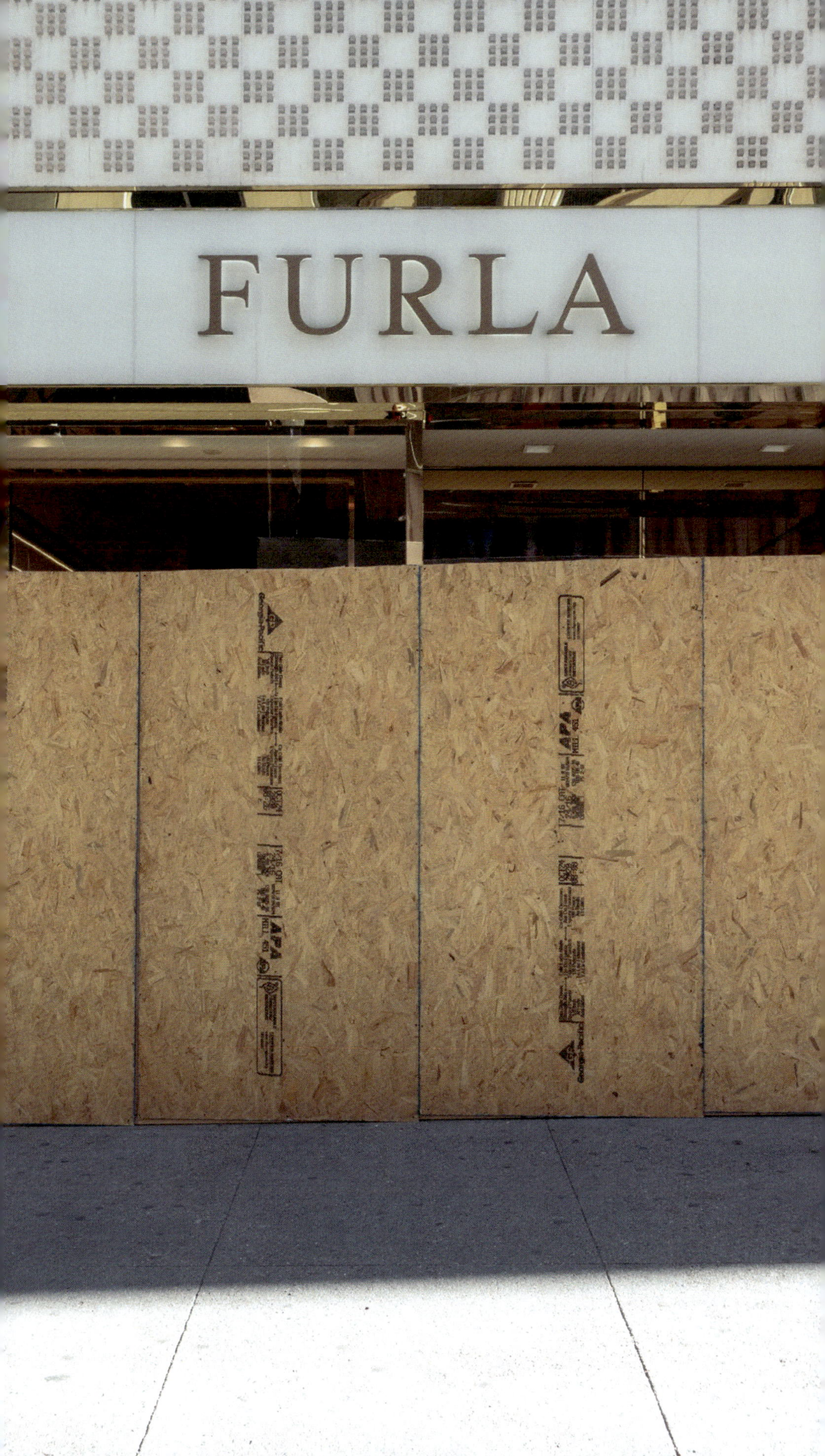
FURLA
APA
APA

November 3, 2020 12:25 PM
645 Fifth Avenue, New York New York, 10022

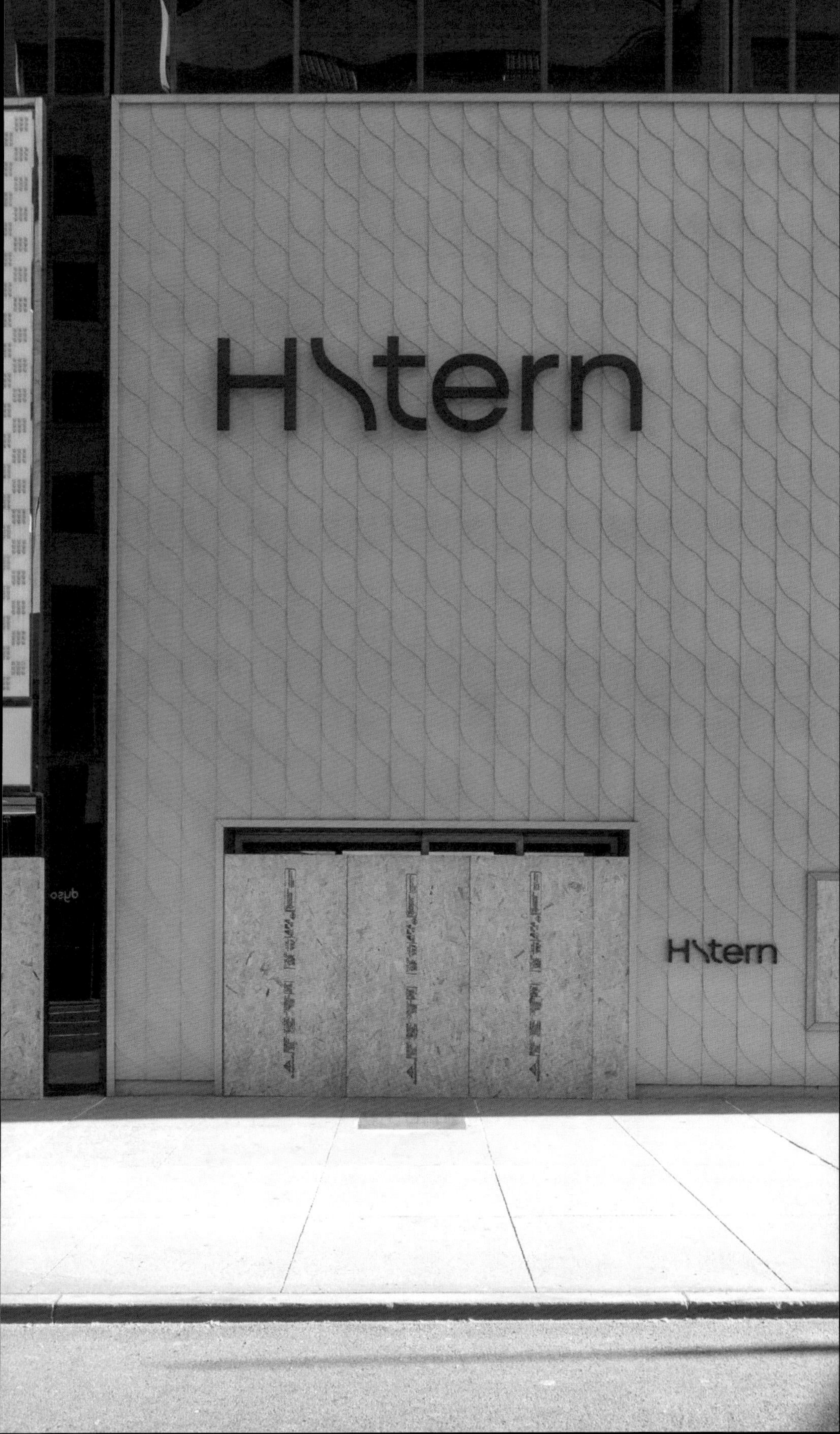

HStern
HStern

November 5, 2020 1:30 PM
116 Greene Street, New York New York, 10012

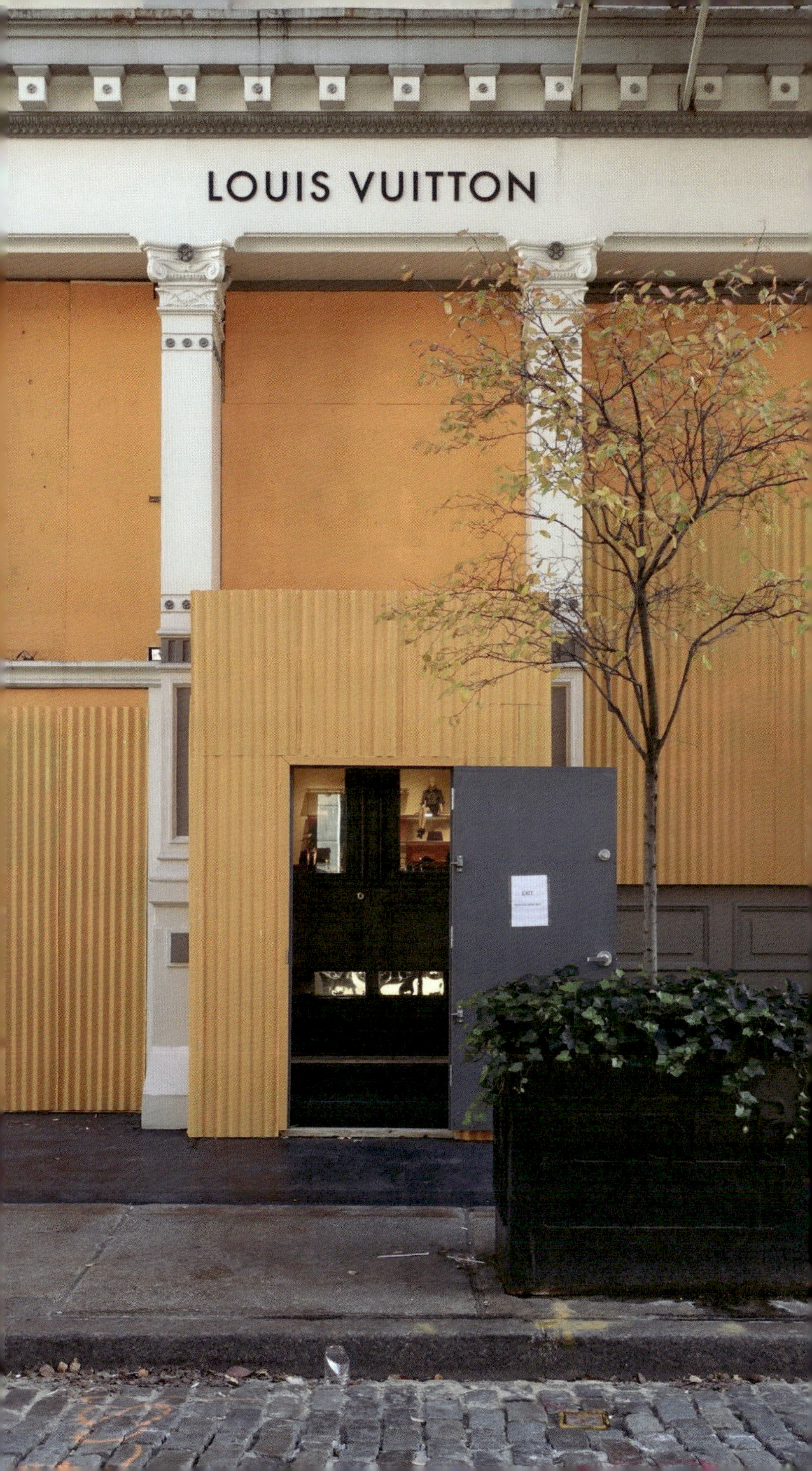
LOUIS VUITTON

November 3, 2020 12:12 PM
730Fifth Ave, New York New York, 10019

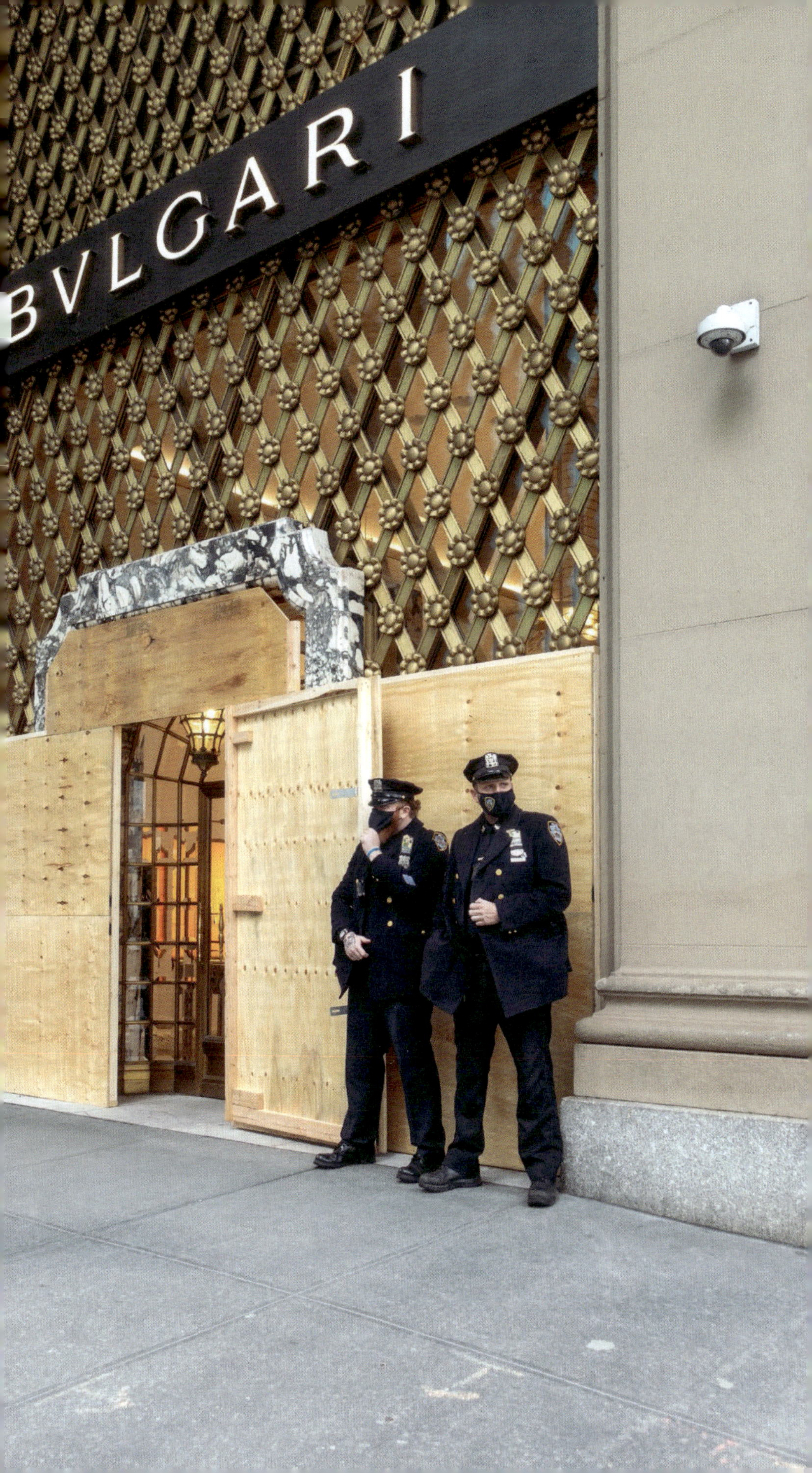
BVLGARI

Unreflective Luxury
Dani Issler

Holly Golightly arrives for Breakfast at Tiffany's during election week 2020, only to find herself confronted with a boarded-up window display. This book is the photographic account of her flânerie.

The untimely representation of luxury brands–whose dazzling aesthetics and iconic style we know so well–momentarily loses its luster in this political landscape. These brands, traditionally anchored in specific Manhattan locations, find their monumental visible status called into question. Around Trump Tower (Fifth Avenue and 57th Street), storefront windows are plastered with plywood panels meant to protect against a gathering storm or an invasion.

The glass window display is essential to the urban idea of luxury; it negotiates the inaccessible interior with the bright, glaring exterior, enticing desire through reflection. In French, **faire du lèche-vitrine** literally translates to "window-licking", a term far more evocative than mere window-shopping.

Here, however, the luxury houses–once eye-candy shrines for passers-by–attempt to shelter in, offering a blind disfigured experience of luxury. While still "open for business", they show no products, just a brand name on the clean, empty sidewalks.

For Adorno, the German term **Schein** ("appearance" or "semblance") explores how things appear to us, often masking deeper realities. His critique examines the tension between appearance and truth, where cultural products like art or media might seem to offer insight, yet often reinforce illusions that obscure social realities. Luxury brands, at this historical moment, offer a rather opaque reality. They do not shine; momentarily liberated from the illusion of the reflective luxurious experience, we are now able to reflect on their "Schein", and ultimately their truth value.

MarieVic's images invite us to playfully observe and comment on the aesthetics of this moment, almost like at a sports match. The power of these brands is divine–they transform plywood into luxury. A Christian encounter? The absent relics of saints send us back to the carpenter's son, and the absence of Schein exposes a sameness among houses that claim authenticity and rarity. Ultimately, their differences are trivial, as appearance and reality exist in a dynamic tension, neither fully separated nor reconciled.

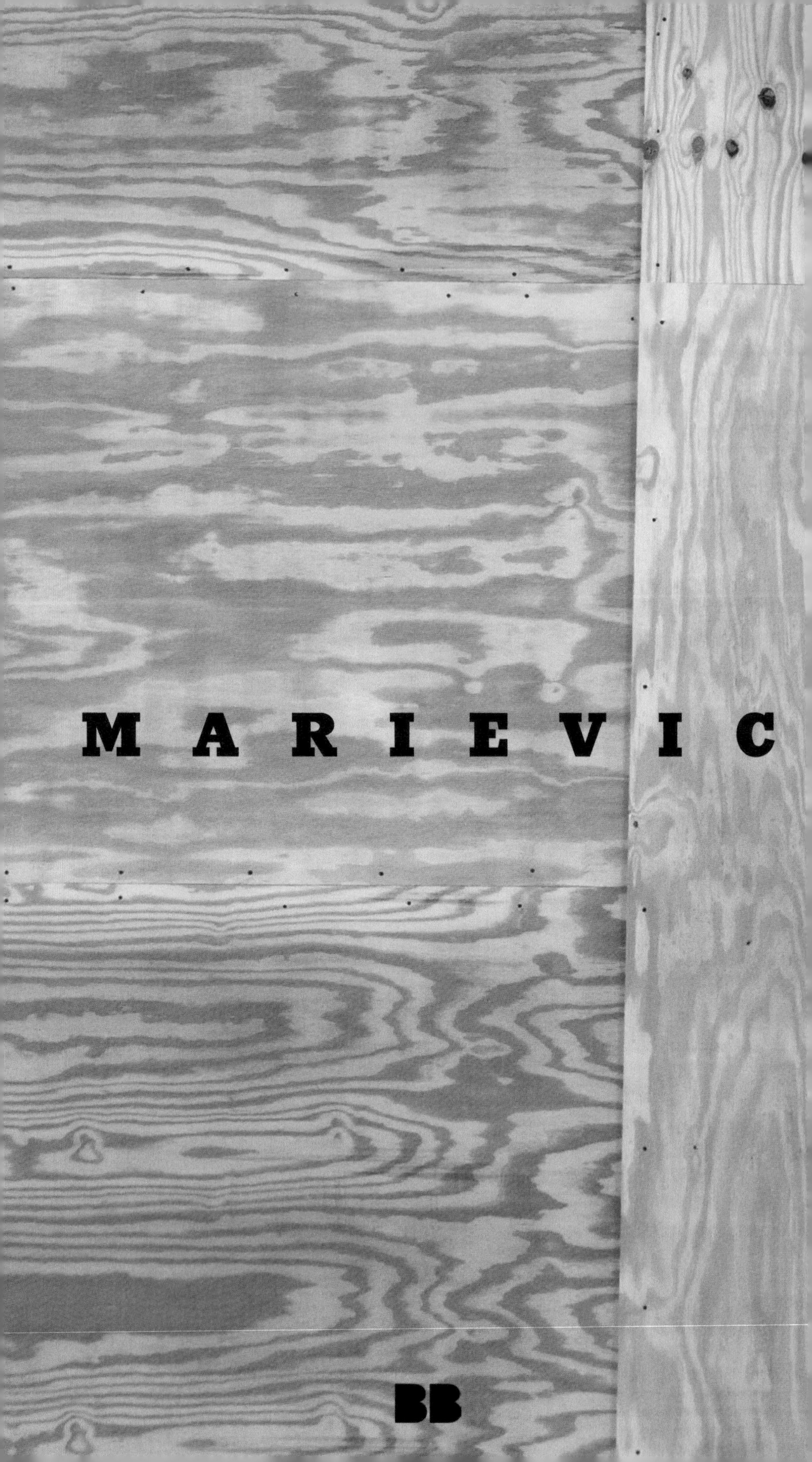
MARIEVIC
BB